MW01274245

Life in Israeli prison

Or

How to live your life in a meaningless world

Ronny Hadad

Copyright © 2020 Ronny Hadad

All rights reserved.

ISBN: 9798550803066

TABLE OF CONTENTS

Introduction..ii

PART I..1

PART II...8

PART III...16

PART IV...24

PART V..32

PART VI...41

PART VII...46

PART VIII..53

PART IX...66

PART X..79

PART XI...97

Epilogue...106

DEDICATION

First and foremost I think I should dedicate this book to myself.

The hell of troubles that I have been through, which made it possible for me to write this book, merits some acknowledgment.

Secondly, to all the cops and jailers that are involved in my story. You deserve a dedication; it might console you when you are in hell.

Introduction

This book is about my experience of Israeli jail as it is in real-life. The book also contains many philosophical discourses with the other inmates: discourses about the meaning of life, politics, religion and more.

In fact, I am not sure whether to count this book as a philosophical work, as a biography or as a plain jail story. It's a blending of all of these together.

The book starts at the hospital after I got shot and arrested.

It continues to describe my daily life in prison, my interactions with the cops and jailers, and of course with the other inmates.

As a philosophical book with a realistic approach this book will give you a lot to think about, this I promise.

PART I

You woke up at 5 am when the guards unlocked the heavy metallic door to your cell. They turn on the light (it can only be turned on or off from outside) and shout "counting time! Wake up! Clothes on! Stand up!" so you need to wake yourself, fast, put on some clothes and stand up.

As soon as you are on your feet the guards leave, slam the heavy door behind them (actually it slams itself) and turn the light off.

You return to sleep – though not necessarily on your bed – your bed is one of two flat metal boards in a double bed, held fast to the side of the wall by iron pins, melted in their ends so no one will pull any part off (and use it to make a sort of a knife). The mattress is a 2 inch thick of a very old, used and dirty sponge.

But alas! This splendid bed is not only yours. A very active colony of bed-bugs, known locally as "bak-baks", is always present. They will bite you day (and especially) night. And though the crashed bodies of the most unfortunate of them litter the walls (smeared with human blood) the colony doesn't find it very hard to replenish its numbers.

That's a very good reason why you might have chosen to sleep on the floor, in the middle of the cell, where the BED-bugs are less disposed to search for human blood.

And indeed, it seems that these little bugs are the terror of even the toughest of their emaciated locked-up snacks.

Well, its 5am and you are somewhat awake. Nothing to do, so maybe going to the toilet to relieve yourself or just fall back to bed (or the floor) and sleep – till 6am when the guards wake you up again. You need to prepare yourself for another day of work, in the prison's factory, or some other job of maintenance inside the prison.

Everything that needs to be done for the prison to function is done by the inmates: from gardening to laundry, fixing and even renovating, painting walls and food making (it doesn't always deserve the appellation of "food") to even being a seller assistant in the prison's cantina – all under strict supervision by the responsible guards of course. Oh yeah, and cleaning too, how could I forget?

Now, you are getting ready for another day of work. You do all the normal things people do when they wake up: toilet, brushing teeth, washing your face, putting jail uniform on (in a bright orange color) and eat something.

For breakfast you get 4 pieces of white bread and 50 grams of white cheese. If you are lucky they serve also a random vegetable, and if you are even luckier it's of a decent quality.

Who serves there delicacies? They are called the "choliya", a privileged group of inmates in every prison wing that is responsible for everything inside the wing: cleaning, food serving, phone-time budgeting for every cell after closing hours, passing orders and complaints between the guards and the inmates, and sometimes they even do feud-management.

The head of the choliya is a person of great importance; he might also inspire some terror (on purpose). He doesn't really lower himself to perform any manual work, like, for example, delivering toilet paper (glass-paper) to every cell once a week, but he rather manages the other "choliya" members and the wing and supposed to also prevent feuds- that's why the guards choose the toughest to be the choliya's head.

Their monthly pay is 40$, BUT they get the best food, and extras, the best rooms (even private rooms) and they are the first to have their cell opened and the last to be closed (it might be 14 hours of opening time for them while only 2 hours for the other inmates).

Just before 7am the cell door was opened. So you will have to be ready at the exit door of the wing where your name will be written on the list of those that come in time. Those that didn't were again waked and warned, and if they didn't feel like working ("I don't feel well") they were sent to the infirmary, to wait up to 8 hours to the doctor in a small congested cell with other inmates, most faking illness, some really unwell. And if you repeat this little trick to avoid work too many times (twice is usually enough) you will be moved to a CLOSED wing.

Now, just before you leave the wing for work you are visited by a paramedic and a guard – if you are one of those that need to be given a medicine every morning.

You are called to the cell's door and are given the pills, and under the watchful eyes of the paramedic and the guard you are to swallow your pills, and then open your mouth and show under your tongue to prove that the pills are not still in your mouth.

These precautions are not without a reason, as many of these drugs are drugs, they are sold and bought among the inmates – and yea, it is still done, actually there is quite a commerce, notwithstanding the guards' precautions. And even the small pill that I now take at home twice daily is worth, in prison currency, one packed of cigarettes. Two of these pills therefore, could be exchanged for a phone card – 6 hours of talking time for 15$. But if you are caught….

Now you are waiting for all the inmates to gather at the exit. The names are on the list and the wing manager gives the order.

The door is opened into a little corridor, all the inmates and some guards enter and the door is closed behind them. Another name check, some shouts and orders and an obedient file of inmates – guards before, behind, and on every side – is herded to work.

You worked for 5-7 hours a day, though if you wanted you could work for more hours in the factories. Your average income would be around 150 to 220 $ per month, and you could use it to buy in the prison's canteen (cigarettes, clean normal water, soap and shampoo, or some proper food. But: 1. you got a fine for the slightest things, a fine that could well amount to your monthly salary and beyond.

2. As the prison's canteen doesn't operate in a free market the prices are highly inflated.

At work you had a supervisor around you and you had to work properly, no sleeping, no fooling around – unless you want to get a fine and to be sent to a closed wing.

But I'm not going to tell you much about work in prison, since I myself never worked there – I was not in a very good medical condition as my captivity had begun by me being shot.

PART II

The bullet entered my lower abdomen from the right and, after a short travel, came out of the back of my left thigh. I was shot from the side, at close range, by a cowardly man.

So I started my captivity at the hospital, guarded by 2 policeman at a time, every watch was 8 hours and an officer came once in a while for an inspection and to feed his cops.

I was in a horrible condition, couldn't even sit or even move.

When I was brought to the hospital it was around 2:30

am. My left leg was completely numb (a nerve was damaged) and I suffered from inner bleeding – the bullet went through my inner organs.

The pain was severe and I felt so weak, I just lay on my back, not moving and hoping it will end quickly: that the doctors will come and sedate me, whether I will wake up later or not didn't seem so important, I just wanted to stop feeling this pain.

But, it seems the doctors were busy (or sleeping). I was handled by the nurses that made some tests and moved me to this machine and to that bed, Here and there talking to me and asking questions – but I was so weak I found it hard to speak.

After some time I was being made ready to being operated upon.

It took some time but after around 2 hours I finally was in the operation room, going to sleep.

When I woke up I was handcuffed to the bed, hands and feet, but I couldn't move anyway. I felt horrible but better. I had tubes here and there around my body and a formidable scar on my abdomen, closed by many little iron pins.

The two cops in attendance have become conscious of my awakening and asked me how I feel.

Well, I felt bad but better. Little did I know that the doctors forgot to put a net when they sewed and clipped me back, what horrible troubles it will cost me…

One of the cops told me that he was present during all of the operation and that he saw everything: "I didn't miss a thing, it was very interesting. I saw how they opened your abdomen and how they clipped it. Don't worry, the doctors were very good but it took so long till the operation begun that we thought that you will die".

The cop said it was a very very long operation; they also looked for the bullet for a very long time and didn't find anything. Apparently they missed the exit wound.

Somewhat later the doctors came for inspection, asking me how I feel and writing some notes. Then a nurse came and gave me some morphine, without asking me whether I wanted it or not. Yea, but I guess I rather wanted it.

That's how my time as a captive in the hospital started. I spent there 9 days, not because I was much better after 9 days (I was more dead than alive) but because the police put some pressure on the hospital management – watching me there took manpower, and also because the health system in Israel, being the way it is, was, hmm, in a state of collapse, so the hospital too was in a hurry to discharge me as soon as possible.

Well after a while I felt more awake, and as there was nothing much for me to do I started talking to the cops.

They mostly talked among them about their income, conditions of work, trivial annoyances with their officers and mostly about the vacation they should receive from work at summer (it was high winter).

It was kind of boring to listen to for hours upon hours so I decided to contribute something more interesting to the conversation.

"What's the time?"

"11:10 AM. how do you feel?"

"Not too good, time doesn't pass."

"You should know that you are lucky to even be alive."

"I do not feel so lucky, my body is in ruins, I have pains, and I'm going to jail. What's so lucky about that? "

"That you are alive, things might get better. You will heal, and people have continued their lives even after jail, and so will you".

"And what's the point in that? I could have died and stopped to exist, it would have been much easier than my current condition."

"Don't say that! You are young and you have every

reason to live. What is your goal in life? "

"What is the goal in life? We live and we die. We are born, go to kindergarten, school, high school, work till we are 70 or more and then become sick and die. What is the goal in all of that? "

"There is no goal except the goal you choose for yourself. Many people are searching for the meaning of life, but they never find it. Many despair and lose all interest in life. What is the meaning of the life of an ant? To support the eco-system? To clean nature's left overs? To annoy us when they search for food at our homes? Ants work all their lives and may get killed, just like that, by some human foot.

So is there no meaning to their lives? Just working and dying? And why work at all?"

"Why indeed? It is pointless. But they do it, they never think whether it's pointless or not."

"Exactly. They don't think of that so it doesn't bother them. And there are people that also don't think about it and just live their lives. They might be happier about it too.

We and the ant and all living things are the same. We live because we live; there is no special goal, no higher plan.

But the vast majority of people MUST have a goal, a higher plan or destiny, a reason why they are alive, beyond randomness and chance.

They cannot find the reason in themselves so they look for a high order, a god, a soul, a war between good and evil. And so they are lying to themselves, believing that the universe was made for them. And if that's not enough they also invented an after-life and souls, another world, and an eternal life. They need to believe in it to avoid a mental, existential crisis. But the truth is that man is just like any other living thing, but in a protected environment. "

"But today there are many people that do not believe in god and eternal life. And still they are not in a crisis. They just live their lives."

"Many are in a crisis, and many just believe in a different lie. How many would admit that they are neither different nor higher than a simple ant? How many can accept that they could die just like ants: suddenly and randomly, without a higher cause or a goal? "

"Not many. I think they don't really think about it when they live their, how did you call it? protected lives.

But what do you mean by protected lives?"

"I mean that their, our, lives are in essence…"

He did not finish. The other watch just came into the room, smiling and greeting their friends. They exchanged a few words, and also a radio, a Taser and a gun, and the first watch went away. I never saw them again.

PART III

The second watch made itself comfortable while the doctors came again, they have decided that the tubes that went inside my nose could be removed and so removed them – you don't want to know how that felt…

Then I spent some restless hours till I got another dose of morphine and slept for a while. When I got up another watch have come, and not long after came the interrogator, he was quite nice, which made me quite suspicious.

He asked me many questions, going round and round, asking the same questions again and again, but his job was quite easy.

I was not ashamed of defending myself (or at least trying) nor saw it as a crime, and after all, the facts were quite clear. I told him what happened as it really has, in a tone of confidence (could you imagine a half dead person talking with a tone of confidence and wonder how it sounds?).

After about an hour he left – and left me exhausted. Not long after one of the cops removed the handcuffs that tied me to the bed, saying it was by the order of the judge – my lawyer was making wonders in the background – and that he must obey, but that he does not agree with it as he thought that I am to be considered dangerous. I asked him, somewhat annoyed, how can I be dangerous when I can't even move out of bed?

And indeed I couldn't appreciate this little freedom at the time, as I didn't and couldn't even move much in my bed anyway.

But the same order said that if I go out of bed I should be handcuffed again, and the cops were happy to oblige when, a few days later I could sit on a chair or a wheel chair.

The next few days have been uneventful. My lawyer

came and explained to me the legal situation – I really didn't care at the time.

When the day came that I finally could be moved out of bed I finally took my first shower since being shot. I was helped to a wheel-chair by the nurses, with some help from the cops, handcuffed to the chair, and then led, by a nice and cheerful person, to the shower. Alas! I couldn't take a shower by myself; I couldn't even take off my clothes. I had to suffer the unfortunate experience of being cleaned like a 2-year-old baby at the age of 31. But I felt refreshed.

After the shower the cops were so very nice that they asked me if I want to go outside (in a wheel-chair) and sit in the sun for a bit. I gladly agreed. Later I discovered that those cops' superiors were not so too very nice – they reprimanded them for their generous initiative.

Finally, after days of being stuck in bed I could see people outside, feel the clean air, and watch the blue cloudless sky (Israeli winter). I felt a bit better. We also had a chat.

"I think I was somewhat ill-treated by the cops that took me captive."

"Why is that?"

"I think that if I was some big criminal or mafia guy I would not have been treated that badly, and so wouldn't have been arrested, not to mention shot."

"Do you know," said one of the cops, "what respect is there between us and the top criminals? They ask us about our families and we ask them about theirs. Every time we come to their homes they offer us something to drink or eat, even opening up a table for us, and if we somehow do something that is against their rights, they comply and then sue us at court with some big-shot lawyer".

You have no idea how much this statement annoyed me, and still annoys me.

"But" says I, "what about simple law abiding citizens,

that do not have a big-shot lawyer to back them? You treat them with much less consideration; some of you are actually like bullies when it comes to simple powerless citizens. You are a terror to normal citizens and a joke to criminals, or even worse, you befriend these criminals, these enemies of society, who it is your job to suppress, not to befriend."

"That's not how it is" said the cop.

"Yes it is"

"No its not"

"Yes it is"

"It's not!"

"You just said it is. And anyway that's not only what I say but what everyone says, people on the street, newspapers, the news... that's why you arc so unpopular."

"We treat anyone as he deserves and do our duty; we respect those that respect us."

"I am sure"

"You can be sure"

"And still I think you and the law treat differently people that have means and power compared to simple citizens that don't."

"Sometimes it does happen that we catch some criminal but the judge is scared and just releases him, it happens too much, and it does hurt our motivation".

"That's really wrong"

We continued quietly, enjoying the sun and the sound of birds till I felt I can't sit anymore and we went back inside.

Sometime after we came back the watch switched again, and shortly afterward came another interrogator, this time one that investigates cops. She explained that, every time a cop shot someone they opened up an interrogation, and so she came to ask for my testimony.

Now, in Israel, those that interrogate cops are also cops themselves, so that's quite explain the statistics that 99% of all charges against cops drop (it's the same kind of system with jailers).

So you won't need any more explanation if I tell you that the interrogator was rough and her questioning hostile. But notwithstanding that, the 2 cops present seemed to have become a little stiff in their demeanor and too obviously obliging towards the interrogator (but she didn't come for them and obviously they knew it quite well).

I told the interrogator (witch) that I don't really care if they sack the cop that shot me or not, so that I really had no interest in that interrogation. She insisted and annoyed me for almost a whole hour – for nothing, because guess what... the charge against the cop was.... Dropped (surprise!).

When the witch... hmm sorry, interrogator, left, I and also the cops felt relieved. After that I had a physiotherapy, which caused some squabbling between the physiotherapist and the cops as they wanted me handcuffed outside bed.

PART IV

My condition was becoming better, after 6 days I slowly started to eat (I lost most of my muscles in these 6 days in hospital).

It was night and I tried to sleep but unfortunately I had the luck of being guarded by a terrible watch.

Two miscreants have decided (by the suggestion of that evening's inspection officer – a miscreant with credentials) that I am too comfortable (yea right!) and so they must need put some difficulties, lest I enjoy myself too much, so they put their radio on high volume and also talkcd loudly among themselves, and refused, insolently refused, to be more quiet. One of them even handcuffed me to the bed saying:

"If you have complaints go to the judge, here I am the judge!" (When he said "judge" I heard "miserable miscreant" – I'm sure that's how he really thought about himself anyway.)

Well, I didn't sleep and so felt my pains increase, but what could I do? I suffered it quietly.

The next watch was completely different, notwithstanding the miscreant advising them to treat me badly they were actually very friendly. One of them saying I had good eyes and asking me how I came to be in this situation.

"You look like a good person, how come you are here?"

"Because I am a good person."

"That can't be"

"It can, had I been a bad scary guy I would have been treated differently".

"But don't you think that what you did is wrong?"

"What's wrong with self-defense? I am a free person (or at least should be) and I have to defend myself against any unjust injury, if I can."

"But you look like such a good person."

"I think I am, but were the cops good or bad?"

"They did their job."

"No, they did not. They are bad people even if they are cops, even worse for betraying their duty. Would you think that just because someone has been given authority he could use it as it pleases him?"

"Of course not"

"Same goes for judges, teachers, civil servants and politicians. If they betray their trust they are the worse of criminals – they are traitors.

A president or a prime minister that uses his authority to benefit himself and abandons the public interest is a criminal and a murderer – just think about how many lives depend on his decisions.

He might act dignified, dress dignified, be surrounded by bodyguards, be driven about in a state car and be saluted with respect – but here is a criminal, the worst of criminals.

How many of our politicians are corrupt? Almost all. And those that aren't corrupt don't succeed in finding their place and sooner or later retire.

Why is it like this?

It is because of our corrupt system, a system that is wrongly called a democracy. At best it's a plutocracy and at worse an oligarchy.

By this system all sort of parasites and cons – expert cons – are draws like flees to warm blood.

They feed their greed and lust for power by using the state, and the public, to serve theirs and their friends' interests.

They have no principles, except money and influence, and by lies – public and shameless lies – double dealings, and pure chicanery do they pursue their goals – unmolested! As the public accept that these are the laws of democracy, these are the rules of the game, and that this is the best form of government possible. IS IT? Of course not. In a democracy the state should serve the people, not the people serve a rich minority.

They tell us that once, in ancient Greece, democracy was direct, but that today a direct democracy is impossible, since we are now millions of citizens and it's impossible to consult us about all those questions of policy that touches us. IS THIS IMPOSSIBLE?

By technological advancement we all have the world in our pockets – the internet, smartphones. Can we not make a more direct democracy by these means?

Will not the citizenry be much better when they know that they decide policy – even just a little of it?

Won't they become much more responsible and involved?

Won't their morals and the state's morals improve?

Instead of just choosing their leaders every few years, among a group of corrupt hagglers, they will choose what is good for them and for THEIR state.

Every leader will be personally responsible for his deeds-

and this alone will scare away all those parasites that now infest our political systems.

And don't tell me about cyber hacking. There is already enough of it and governments handle it with their own cyber units".

"Yea we have cyber units in the police, the very best work there."

"Yes of course. What I suggest is completely feasible, but the people will have to demand it. Don't expect the parasites in government to give up any of their influence or leave us in peace on their own accord.

Don't our people have a goal that they want and can achieve? Of course they have, but they will need to fight for it."

"Fight who?"

"Their enemies. Including their dignified and well-dressed enemies. Their corrupt leaders are their current worse enemies."

"And will they fight?"

"No! They are too comfortable in their liberal slavery. They will only fight when they face some catastrophe, probably an economic catastrophe."

"Perhaps. Let's hope we won't get there. But what do you mean by "liberal slavery"? "

"I mean, that we work all our lives. When we are young we are being prepared, trained, for work. And we are governed from above; we don't have a real part in our government.

But we get bonuses – vacations abroad, the right and possibility to (little by little) improve our material circumstances – housing, cars, clothes, furniture, and electronic appliances.

Also we have the possibility to have fun (after work, of course), clubs, bars, restaurants, parties, music, but eventually all this makes us hedonistic and docile – the perfect slaves – happy slaves. But we are not really happy.

We have a hole inside us, something is gnawing us from the inside and we don't know what it is – it is our wish for something meaningful – to do something meaningful with our lives."

This chat continued for a bit more, till the next watch came. The cops of the previous watch left, not before saying they won't mind to talk for hours like this.

The next day I was interrogated again, this time even more extensively – apparently they couldn't trust my first interrogation since I was, well, half dead and on morphine, but my condition improved and though my left leg was still paralyzed I could somewhat walk.

So after 9 days in hospital the day came that I was released, though still in a very bad condition.

But I was released from hospital to prison.

PART V

I was wearing hospital clothes, sitting on a chair, waiting for a police car to take us to the police station – as always, the simplest things were too complicated for out very competent police force. So we waited… it was a hard waiting.

Finally we drove away; it wasn't a long drive to the station.

There, I was asked how do I feel, and was put on a chair while the officers got busy with paper work.

While I waited a very special person came in- a nutcase. He was arrested running wildly with a knife on the streets.

He was a believing man and believed with his all heart that god will punish the cops that arrested him. He shot out a train of words, with occasional loud eccentric laughter, filler with invectives, stuff from science fiction, conspiracies, prayers and curses.

The cops suffered him with practiced patience, a thing that made it quite clear to me: I was going to meet more lunies in the very near future (alas, I was very unfortunately right! Very right indeed).

Well, I signed a few papers and off we went – to bring me into prison.

All this driving and moving was very hard for me and because of my condition I was brought to a prison wing that was a mix between a medical center and a prison – I was there for a total of 3 months.

When we entered the prison complex the guard looked at me and asked the cops, in wonder, "is HE going to prison?"

We went through some paper work, photography, and a search till I finally entered the facility. I was put in the wing of the severely disabled for my first week there and immediately checked by a doctor on my arrival.

I was put in a room with 3 old men and a young man from the Philippines, whose job there was to take care of the disabled under his care.

The room was better than the one in hospital, with a TV, air conditioner, wooden closets and hospital beds. The wooden closets were filled with snacks, so jail wasn't so bad wasn't it?

This place was considered like a hotel in prison. There was even a variety of food. And milk! And milk products! And jam! And more than 1 fruit or vegetable a day.

But for some of the people there it was their last stop, before death.

The old men were actually quite funny as they argued and teased each other, but I talked most with the young man from the Philippines. He told me about his country and his life, about his wife and children and how he came to Israel to earn enough money to support them. When night came we had a little chat:

"Do you have any wife or children?" he asked.

"No, I'm still a child myself, and anyway I don't think I want to have children or marry."

"Why not?"

"Why should I? That's such a responsibility and also I think it's somewhat immoral to make children."

"Immoral, how?"

"Well, whoever is born must also die, is dying pleasant? Unborn people don't die and don't feel pain."

"I didn't think of it like that before, but yeah I guess you are right".

"You know, when I was young and first heard about hell and how slippery our road to heaven is I was shocked! How could my parents be so irresponsible as to create me just because they felt like having a child, like a child that wants a dog, and not thinking of risking the possibility of their child not only dying but experiencing long tortures in an afterlife !

Now I know the only hell there is, is here in this world,

but still, even people with better lives than myself have to feel pain, grief, disappointment, boredness and the like."

"But there are also good things to experience."

"there are, but good experiences are a minority in our lives - yes, even ours that live under a democracy of sorts and have material benefits to make our life comfortable: food in plenty, electricity, housing… also we have our spare time and hobbies, we are not lab animals - who suffer horribly, nor are we cage animals raised for slaughter or entertainment, nor again are we some primitive tribesmen or people that struggle to exist in the third world.

And anyway what are good experiences to something that is unborn, that does not exist? Nothing. Can you tempt a rock to feel because it can enjoy something? No, it's absurd. But when we suffer you could well wish to be like a rock, unfeeling."

"So, do you say that all life is bad and we should all not exist?"

"It would have been better to us had we not existed, but

we do. And as we do we better make use of our lives."

"What use?"

"Have a goal, enjoy life as much as possible, and try to accomplish that which we desire."

"So you are in favor or against life?"

"Neither, I think in a practical way. We live, so let's live well, as best we can."

"But then if we better not exist what's the point in living?"

"There is no point, but we are here. So the only thing we can do is to live, or die. And if we live we do so to accomplish our goals, the goals we set to ourselves – that is our meaning of life. "

"And yet you say we shouldn't make children."

"So I do. They do not yet exist; there is no reason to bring them to die"

"Say what you will, I believe, and so does everyone else,

that we must have children, families. That's our meaning of life; we must procreate and pass our heritage on. "

"Why?"

"Because that's what people always did, if we won't procreate there won't be people left in the world".

"So what?"

"Don't you care if there won't be people on earth, our continuation?"

"No, I am a practical man. I won't know these people and they won't know me. I don't care if after I die there won't be any people left, why should I care? And what should they exist for? Wars, poverty, plagues, slavery, car accidents? It would be also good for them not to exist."

"Say what you will, you have no kids. When you have a child and hold it in your arms you will understand, this child will give meaning and purpose to your life."

"Perhaps. But what good can it give him? Has anyone ever given a thought to this question?"

Next morning I was taken to the court, just a routine business of legally prolonging my arrest (captivity).

Since the jailers didn't agree to take me there on a short notice the police had to do it, though they had an hour drive to reach the prison complex. For some reason the police and the jailers detest each other, and won't miss any opportunity to annoy each other – perhaps they should give a thought to the fact that they should be allies, since both are detested by the public.

I was taken at 6am, chained, in a police car. When arriving at the court building we were searched (and the policemen were searched upon too) and I was put in a small dirty room with an unwalled toilet with another 10 or more prisoners. Some slept on the dirty floor some on stone benches, some talked, some talked nonsense.

I have found out, with consternation, that we can wait there till afternoon, till everyone was brought before the judge- and all this waiting just for a few minutes of some formal procedure.

There were some 5-7 more cells so it took time. Luckily for me(in a way) since I was in such a bad condition I waited only for 2.5 hours, and after I finished this little procedure I waited only another half an hour before I was on my way back to prison.

PART VI

I came back in time for lunch and sat on the only chair left unoccupied. I greeted the 2 people that sat there, one of them later became a close friend, though we had our arguing- he wasn't an easy person.

While talking with them and listening I found out that both were killers, my future friend have been a past mafia hitman, now serving his second life sentence.

They asked for the reason of my captivity and I asked theirs, both were already old and infirm and they seem to have instantly liked me. They told me some stories and I told them about me. It was funny but when I told them that I know that animals are better than people they smiled, saying "all killers love animals" – meaning I had a potential- that was supposed to be a compliment.

Notwithstanding their pride in their profession they also

told me about using drugs since the faces of the men they killed were still hunting them – something I couldn't understand, I guess that's because they kill for money or some silly arguments.

But, is killing people can be generalized as a crime? Why so? When innocent living creatures get killed, in a cruel way, for meat, experimentation, skins… or for no reason, like poisoning insects and mice that just want to live their lives, putting stick traps… isn't that a crime?

Or is just killing people a crime?

But we can kill mass murderers, we kill in war. Is killing bad people wrong? Why so?

Is killing innocent animals and torturing them is ok? If someone kills animals, have no compassion for their suffering, but helps people – is he a good person?

I think – actually I know – that hurting living things is wrong, it's evil. Does it matter that they are from our own or from a different species? Experience shows that our worse enemies are from our own species.

I don't understand those that say that people's lives are

holy. Bad people are bad people, what is so holy about them?

Should we, for example, save the life of a stranger that might have wronged us, cheated us, that care only for his life, instead of saving the life of a dog that might have given his own life to protect us and our family? Will such behavior be considered reasonable?

Is it because humans are so advanced? At least compared to other species on earth?

But most people I met were quite silly; if it was up to them we would still be in the Stone Age. It's only a fraction, a very small fraction, of humanity that invents new things, and they improve because they have and they build upon the knowledge of their predecessors. But most of us are quite simple. I would not even know how to make the paper that I write upon or the pen I write with.

And anyway, being more advanced doesn't mean being better.

Think of that, how many bad and lowly things do humans practice that other species are not guilty of. Like:

gambling, greed, murder for no reason, sadism, masochism, child abuse, child murder, rape, parents killing and raping their own children, drugs, alcohol, cigarettes, pornography, also in its milder form in commercials, reality shows, TV, food addictions, bulimia, coach potatoes, mental disturbances and phobias, vanity and jealousy, envy, hatred.

All these things are quite unique to people, and they definitely don't make us better than other species.

And even if we were better, does that give us the right to tyrannize over those less advanced? If the answer is yes then slavery is ok, then the Nazis were right, then all those primitive tribes that were wiped out for their territory were justly slaughtered.

But you might say, no, these are people, people have rights. Who gave us there "rights"? We! We gave them to ourselves!

Now imagine that, by the same logic and morality that our life is precious because we are so advanced - a higher form of extraterrestrial life come here (which alone will show us that they are more advanced than us) and slaughter us for space and use us as they see fit.

Would you justify that? Would you agree and say that they are right? That they, being much more advanced than us, they can do with us as they will, that their lives are more precious than our own? I guess you won't agree to that.

You will call them evil just because they will do to you what you yourselves do to other animals – to others.

We ate and talked and those killers didn't seem evil to me, they were quite nice and talked and laughed like any other people I knew. So what's the difference?

PART VII

A few days passed till the day came when I felt good enough that I didn't need much help in daily functions, so the paramedics told me that next day I'll be moved to another wing (in the upper floor) where the people are somewhat more alive. In my last night in this wing I was in my room, together with the old men and the young man from the Philippines, watching TV.

"So what is the government system in your country?" I asked.

"It's a republic"

"Is it liberal and free?"

"Yes but somewhat less than here"

"Here too the government is not that liberal, unless you are rich."

"That's how it is everywhere."

"Yes, true. And I think it's going to get worse all over the world in the future."

"Why is that?"

"Because I see inequality rising, and rising rapidly, and on the other hand I see governments become stronger and more in control of our daily life- cameras everywhere, every action is registered, our use of technology that compromises out privacy – all that mean we can and are being monitored by governmental bodies and agencies. And when governments gain such power and abilities they will use it- for the advantage of a few."

"That won't happen, there are so many democracies, it's the age of democracy, and people have rights, and the people still have power- the government needs the people."

"Is that so? Not so long ago people had very few rights and governments had absolute control, but when total war came governments needed ALL people to fight – to help in the war effort. And when they needed people to fight they had to concede more and more rights and freedoms. But NOW, with weapons so advanced that mass armies are a thing of the past, governments won't need us to fight, and so will keep us unarmed and docile while milking us for work and taxes. Also, these governments are much stronger than primitive governments – now a high degree of absolute control is possible, down to your most private actions – the government will know where you live and when you went yesterday, what you eat, where you drive , who you know and talk to, and what's your thoughts(if you talk loudly or share them via social media), everything about you is known, and used, it's just a matter of time till it will be despotically used."

It is used, but not for making us slaves. We still do have rights and freedoms."

"Yes we do, but we are not equal and the rich and powerful enjoy their rights, their rights are respected, while ours are often trampled under foot.

There are too many examples. Even us here- had we been rich we might not have been here, I would defiantly not have been shot and then put in prison so unjustly, it would have been completely different had the police faced someone rich and known.

And even if some influential person does go to prison, which is rare, he gets much less time, and much better conditions and treatment.

And this unjust and unequal tendency is just getting more common that even simple people take it for granted and don't even stir to protest- that is the road for tyranny".

"Still, if you work hard you can be better off; you have an opportunity to be rich".

"You do, but I think that in time being rich and powerful will be limited to a few, we already see that, here in Israel, and much in the USA.

But even if we still have opportunities to get rich, so what? What about those (the majority) that are not so good with money, should they be slaves? Are they of less quality than money loving people?

Those rich capitalists believe that it's a matter of evolution – Darwinism. That they are the fittest to survive and the rest of humanity belongs to some slavish, poor and unfit class. What nonsense! Just look at these capitalists, are they the wonder of creation? Far from it. I can't believe they are. They have their qualities and under a capitalistic system they flower, but if different qualities of strength be needed to survive they might find themselves unfit. Of course the capitalists are useful and productive, but they are not the flower of humanity.

I admire their inventiveness and resourcefulness in business, but there are other qualities that I admire even more, like goodness, honesty, loyalty- qualities that many of the poor might have in abundance. Why then should they be slaves? Just because they do not excel in the capitalist game?

They might work hard and honestly all their lives, but still remain humble compared to the very rich. And they are used- for work, service and taxes. They are the backbone of the state but they are treated with contemp."

"This is true" said one of the old men, " I have been working all my life, payed taxes, served in the military, but I see it with my own eyes and feel it on my flesh, only money and power counts, we count as nothing, as expendables. Some 50 years ago it was not so- we had ideals, we worked in common to reach these ideals, of course money and power played a role then, but not like this- people were still more important."

"Maybe it is because there are more people" said the young man.

"Yea, these changes are in a vast measure due to human population explosion. The social, economic and political spheres undergo much tension and obvious deterioration. But what can one do? There is no practical way to control it and we are heading towards disaster, how many give this fact a thought? The imminent danger of a destructive war due to mounting pressure, economic crisis, plagues that can't be contained or controlled. All this can come upon us every day.

We are 8 billion humans on earth, in 20 years we should be 16 billions – can we support this? No, too much tension, it will come to an explosion."

"You are very pessimistic you know that?"

"No, just practical- I see what is obvious, what everyone should know but what everyone disregard, they continue as if nothing is going to happen... "16,000,000,000 people, yea we can handle it, there will be enough food". Food? Maybe, but there would be an awesome deterioration in living conditions, friction, crime, tension between states. That's why I don't think democracy will hold in the future".

"That's your problem" said the old man laughing.

"Yea, we are in for it..."

PART VIII

Early morning I was waked up and told to gather my belongings (not much to gather). I said goodbye to my roommates and followed the guards.

We used the elevator to go up to the upper floor. I was given a room for non-smokers. Only 2 men were in the room, both on wheel chairs, both murderers. One was around 50 years old the other 75. They already were 5 years in this same room with each other, and hated each other's guts.

The room was less tidy than in the lower floor, actually this entire wing was less tidy. The people here, though some on wheel chairs, were active, and took care of themselves.

This wing, like the previous one, was quite small; there

was a short corridor, with 6 cells on each side and steel bars as an entrance gate. Close to the entrance there was the dining room, which was also a club – people sat and played, talked or watched TV. There were chairs and tables there.

The dining room also had an exit to the "yard" (it was more like a balcony with bars), there you had a small place to walk and exercise (if you could) and catch some sun (which you barely see).

The inmates favorite pass time was playing remmicubes, and sometimes gambling on the score. I never bothered to learn the game's rules.

This wing's doctor was a rough lady, but she could also be nice.

So, I was in my new room organizing my bed and the little clothes I had and went with one of my roommates to the dining room. In the dining room they said one name repeatedly, "Halabi", I asked who he was. My roommate said he was one that complained a lot, though some people said he used to be tough - he killed 7 men (at least he was sentenced for only 7) and got 7 life sentences+20 years. He was not to leave this place and he knew it.

I was curious and wanted to see him. "Very well" said my roommate "we will wait for him and I will give you a hint when it's he that comes".

Some while later an old man on a wheel chair entered the dining room, he had a silly childish expression, it was Halabi.

"What? This one a killer? Killed 7 people? Really? He doesn't look like a killer."

"Killers never look the part, and the more they don't look it the more dangerous they are."

"Incredible, and what about Malik, he looks like a murderer."

"But he isn't, I tell you, murderers don't look like murderers."

"And why do you think it's like that?"

"It is because they don't see themselves as murderers, so their face doesn't get any harsh features, like the features you would expect a murderer to have.

We look like being something only if we are conscious of being that something, if it gnaws at us, if we reproach ourselves for it, then our features and demeanor may change accordingly, but if we see ourselves as innocent then we will not see ourselves as evil and so won't be seen as evil externally.

We all kill insects for example, and eat flesh, but we don't feel bad about it or feel that we have done something wrong - but if we are aware that killing animals is killing, like killing people, then we see ourselves as murderers, as doing something that is wrong, and so we will also look like murderers."

"Yea, I guess that's true. So it means that many that kill people don't feel sorry for it?"

"They believe that they have killed someone that deserved to die, and they, being in prison for it, feel wronged, so they see themselves as the innocent side.

Not everyone here think they are innocent, but many do. And after all I too believe that killing people isn't always wrong. There are bad people, why should they not be killed?"

"Well, it's unlawful."

"It is, I am well aware of it, but morally it's not always wrong. Murderers may be more practical than many wise men – killing is killing, you kill a bear, a bee, a bird, you may as well kill a person- it's all the same".

"Not everyone, actually almost no one, thinks that that's the same thing, they say that human life is sacred."

"Yea right. That we are humans doesn't mean we shouldn't kill humans. Our worse enemies are people; a bee can't hurt you or betray you as a human can. And besides, in nature it is also like that – the worst fights are among the individuals of the same species."

"Yea that is true, if I have enemies, if someone did me any wrong it was always a person, and certainly not a person with a sacred life. Still, I won't kill them."

"But sometimes you just might or you have to. Is that so

wrong? Is that unnatural or unreasonable? And are not enemies in war also humans? And terrorists are they not humans?"

My roommate had a compelling eloquence. We talked a bit more until I got back to my room. There I saw the former hitman from the other wing - he too was transferred here.

I greeted him and we had a little chat. Then we had our dinner, watched TV, and talked till we have fallen asleep. And so ended my first day in this new wing.

After a week in the same room - which was now full - a new guy came, also a non-smoker (in prison non-smokers were a unique species).

Since he couldn't be with smokers and our non-smoking room was full, I was asked to move to another room, only me and him - since no one was allowed to be alone in a room.

I didn't have much choice but to agree.

My new roommate was in his 40's, a family man, he was no criminal and all this jail experience was new and scary for him- and I could well understand him. He had children and a wife and said that he was imprisoned for a false charge – a matter involving money.

All this came as a shock to him, in the middle of his everyday life it came upon him from nowhere.

That's why he was very agitated and asked me a lot of questions concerning this jail and it's routine. I told him that this place can be barely considered a jail, though you are locked up, and that we are lucky that we are not in a real jail – where the conditions are much worse.

My words seemed to make him more relaxed and then more nervous. Well, he was a decent fellow.

After making himself comfortable in his room he went to

make a phone call to his family (the phones were outside the rooms, in the hall. They were like the old public phones, before cell-phones came out). He seems to have become over-excited by talking to his family again – he cried – which caused some talking, amazement, and much attention. Well, you couldn't really blame him, though some did.

I was in my room and I knew about this only because when he entered the room some of the inmates followed him, telling him it's wrong to cry like this, especially so publicly in front of everyone – some even entered the room sitting beside him and talked with him about how out of place it was. But he repeated it the day following.

I guess the inmates took it so seriously because they also felt like crying, but they didn't dare – so they thought others shouldn't dare as well.

"I just couldn't hold myself, you know, when I heard my young son's voice and the way he asked me when I'm going to return home. And my wife has taken all this very seriously and doesn't leave the house. You know how hard it is, and it just came from nowhere, just out of the blue.

I was supposed to have a kidney transplantation abroad too, perhaps you saw me on TV – my friends made a contribution campaign on my behalf (my new roommate was a high ranking firefighter – and saved many lives in the course of his career). All was ready, and suddenly this happened – just because of money – of greed."

"Yea, many troubles come because of money, everyone wants more and more of it, it's very dominant in our culture – moneymaking, spending, and materialism."

"Yes, people will do everything for money – whether right or wrong."

"But money isn't a bad thing – it's a very efficient means of exchange. It's better than clumsy bartering and it's a comfortable currency for trade. The problem is greed."

"And yet wanting more money is what motivates people to work, to contribute to society – it's what makes roads, cars, electricity, consumer good, and a variety of different articles available for us from around the world a possibility. Without capitalism there would be much less of all these enterprises that benefit humanity.

The root of evil here is when people try to get rich by unfair means, without contributing anything to society. That's when wanting more money is called greed - to want more than you deserve."

"So true. That's another good thing that people found a way to turn into a bad thing, into a disease."

"You are right, but that's human nature it seems. Even the idea of socialism – which is a beautiful idea – has become communism, a bloodbath of corruption."

"People – some people – can have beautiful ideas, utopic ideas, for the good of humanity, but when they try to implement them they need to make many compromises. And even then the people that should help make this idea into reality often think only of benefiting themselves, especially if they get some power, and so, sooner or later, every ideal idea that is being made into reality sinks to the natural level of human nature, of the crude, egotistic nature of most people.

I wonder if any beautiful idea of society could ever

become a reality, without being corrupted."

"Probably not, unfortunately."

We ended our conversation with this pessimistic conclusion.

The following day something unfortunate happened. An old man, with diapers, very very unclean, and smoking like a chimney was put in our room. It was horrible. He didn't shower and he always shouted and smoked. Whatever he ate dripped to his chin and stuck to his short gray beard, he didn't bother to clean even his face.

He annoyed everyone and had the uncommon talent of making those around him feel miserable.

My roommate was always mad when he smoked (it being a non-smoking room) and argued with, and yelled on, this accursed wretch.

So the old man agreed he won't smoke inside the room, but as soon as my roommate took a nap he would smoke as many cigarettes as he could, till my roommate would choke and cough himself awake, and with a red face and a furious tone yell "you smoke again?! What have I told you about smoking in our room?!"

"I was not smoking!" he hid the cigarette.

"So why did I see a damn cigarette in your mouth?"

"It was off, I don't have a lighter."

"Are you nuts? The whole room is filled with smoke."

"Not me."

"Ok, but don't smoke here again" he says, going to the bathroom.

"What the hell! What have you done in the bathroom?! You can't even..."

I better stop here.

Well after a weekend of smoke and disgust he was moved to another wing (thank goodness) but I was left traumatized. Promising myself I won't let people of this sort to be put with me in the same room again. But alas!

This promise was not kept.

PART IX

The days passed. The former hitman annoyed everyone, including me – he was too energetic, messy and chaotic.

Out room received a new guest, again only for the weekend, an 18 years old boy. He was looking quite nice and innocent, but alas, when I talked with him it was clear his mind has sunk deep into the crime world. It was a sad thing to witness in someone so young that might have been a good young man.

He told me that he grew up on the names of some of the heads of crime syndicates, people that ended either being assassinated or committed suicide, or were rotting in jail. I was shocked, were these people really his role models?

I did not know much about the crime world and its mentality, it seemed strange to me to admire such people and wishing to lead such a life.

"So why not quit this nonsense and start a new life?" I asked.

"What for? Its ok, I know how to stay out of troubles."

"But you are in jail."

"Yeah but this is my first time and I could have avoided it if I wanted. Actually I am here because I did not want to frame a friend, but I know how to play it smart and stay out of troubles."

"So you never were in any troubles with the law before?"

"No, and I did almost every imaginable thing."

"Really?"

"Really! I once almost killed someone. He didn't payed me so I hit him with a car."

"Did he not go to the police?"

"No he didn't, and anyway he couldn't prove anything."

"But in the end you will get into troubles."

"Not if I play it smart, and I know how to play it smart."

"Still, won't it be better not to live such a life?"

"This is life. You have to be strong to survive, if you show any weakness people will take advantage of you, and then you lose everything."

"That's partly true, but still you don't need to be strong all the time, like in old times, like in nature – we live in a society and things are different."

"Things are the same; we are still animals by nature. Society is an artificial environment. If you look at things correctly you will see that we live in a ruthless world and you have to be strong to survive."

"I see the people that stand high in society, not all of them are strong and they still succeed."

"You are wrong, they don't need to be violent to be strong, they are still ruthless, they do what is necessary for them to stay on top – they don't let any feelings of sympathy, or even the law, to stand in their way."

"And how come they are not in prison?"

"some end up in prison, but most know how to play it for their own advantage, they change the laws to suit them, they find subterfuge in the laws, they use lobbying and personal connections, either to change the laws or to make it so that they will be more favorable to them or to avoid being detected when they break the law to their own advantage, and they usually succeed.

There is the illusion that we live in a peaceful and equitable society, but that's only an illusion. Behind closed doors it's the strong and unscrupulous members of society that run things, it is they who reap the benefits of society and this is so while we work hard for them, and most of the time we are not even aware of it."

"You have some point, but does it mean we all need to be ruthless and unscrupulous to survive?"

"Maybe not to survive but to succeed and to live well. If we play by the rules of the strong we are their slaves. Do you want to be a slave?

I know I don't. I prefer to follow my own rules and to be the master rather than the slave."

"But you won't necessarily succeed."

"No, but I fight, I fight to be on top, I was not born to be a slave and I won't accept a life of cowardice and slavery. I will make my own rules and follow them. All those people who have made it to the top had a slight regard to the rules, they followed only the rules that served them best."

"That's a cynical way to look at things."

"But that's how things are."

So we ended our conversation, and I got a lot to think about: he did have some point after all.

A few days later the kid also left and I and my roommate were left alone again.

After a few days both of us were moved to a different room (to save space) and our previous room was closed and locked.

We had another roommate there, an elderly one, but he was released a few days after we arrived. The elderly man had a friend, a younger man, that came to visit us in our room and sit with us for a while, after his elderly friend got out he still came for me and we became friends.

His own room was secluded from the other rooms, and his wing was at the other side of the guards' room.

There the inmates had their own rooms, for various reasons: such as bad behavior or a feud with someone, but most of them were allowed to get out of their wing to visit their friends and stay at the club\dining room and play and talk. My new friend had been here for more than 2 decades and had another decade to go- he didn't get a third down from his sentence; the committee decided that he was capable of kidnapping a guard – absurd!

We passed another few days alone, me and my roommate. I played a bit of game boards with the other inmates, watched TV, read some books and taking it easy. Except from suffering horrible and unending pains in my left leg (a nerve was hurt), and barely being able to sleep because of the pain, everything was great.

Then an elderly man, 90 years old, came to our room, straight from hospital. He could barely walk.

He was very dirty, had a strong smell of urine and looked very weak. When trying to take a shower by himself he did fall and bled a bit.

Later he told us how, when in hospital, he was treated outrageously by the guards. Being handcuffed to his bed for 2 weeks! He was not even always allowed to go to the toilet (hence the smell of urine).

We were shocked to hear how the jailers had treated him (90 years old man!). Was this really moral? It certainly was lawful, but moral?

When the old man told us how he was treated he had tears in his eyes – it was just horrible.

Next day, my new friend came to visit us in our room, I told him about the old man and told him his story, the old man confirming and expanding (again with tears in his eyes). My friend was obviously outraged.

"And is this justice to treat an old man like this? These jailers and cops are supposedly the keepers of justice, but what they do is immoral."

"Many things about the laws of the state and the way they are enforced are immoral. This is known to everyone, that for the privileged the laws are not as rigorous as for the rest of the people."

"Yes, in the end the state laws only serve the privileged. Take taxes for example. The simple man that lives by his work has to pay his taxes to their full and on time, even if paying them means he won't be able to finish the month. And if he is late in paying or has inadvertently forgot to report on some small earnings then he is mercilessly fined – so that his humble means are even more reduced for him and for his family. And we are taught that paying tax is the "right thing to do", it's the law, whoever is not paying tax is a thief, a thief that steal from me and from you – and people actually believe in it! People even go and report on one another. But while this is the law for the simple, law abiding, citizen the rich have another arrangement.

According to the doubtful reason of encouraging the economy the rich get huge discounts on their taxes, if they pay them at all. If they don't pay the amount that they owe to the state it is relinquished anyway. And this is while the simple citizen has to pay everything and in time!

The rich also have many subterfuges, so that they can avoid paying taxes or pay a much smaller percentage of their earnings than me and you. And is that moral? That while those that struggle everyday so that they could afford food, clothing and housing should pay a higher, much higher, percentage of their income to the state while those that have millions and billions should receive discounts, should have their dues postponed or even deleted?

Everyone should know that this is not justice – but that's the law, and no one seems to really question this law."

"Yea I wonder what's going on with the people. They all know this (they watch a lot of news broadcasts and read newspapers), but they complain and nevertheless pay. They don't act. Neither on this nor on nothing else. This inequality before the law, under supposedly democratic regimes, doesn't seem to bother them much - they accept it and they take democracy for granted."

"People should know that they need to always keep fighting to keep real democracy alive, if they don't then they will gradually lose it, as is happening now."

"The problem is that the people don't really have someone to rally behind. All their leaders are busier enriching themselves rather that fighting for the benefit of the people and democracy. By doing so they betray their trust - a huge crime, but completely legal. People know politicians for what they are, and know how they work - but they are ready to accept that as the norm and so, bartering the public good and the public interest for money, position, power and other base interests, is accepted by the public as a lawful way to rule and make things done in a democracy. That's just unbelievable."

"Yea, the problem is that there is not a champion of the people, of democracy, but there are many champions of self-interest and inequality."

"People should really fight; fight for their rights and for the state. It is not good to have the laws of the state to be in the charge of corrupt men.

They have their laws and we have ours. Look at us, we are in prison, some of us for trivial things, and even people that are here for bigger stuff, like drug dealing and murder- they feel the full rigor of the law. But when those high-ups steal or deal wrongly with public money and interests, or even with people's lives, health and livelihood, when in wars or by unpreparedness for disasters they are responsible for countless murders by their corrupt blunders - do they pay for it?"

"No they don't", my friend sighted, " even if they are caught (and many don't get caught, they can evade the laws easily, being the ones who write the laws or the friends and family of those that do), they get such light sentences."

"Yea, if you are a simple man from among the people and you won't pay the comparatively little (in state standards) taxes you "owe" you will be mercilessly put in prison and fined so highly that you will be left with only debts. But if you are from among the privileged (big business, politicians, high ranking public SERVANTS and the like) you can steal and cheat , all you will get will be a short sentence (if you get anything at all) and a small fine. So that it actually pays to steal even if you are caught, as long as you steal big."

"And that's our immoral law for you. And even if some of the privileged do go to jail they get VIP style conditions – so that they actually live better in jail than simple people live their lives out of it."

"How absurd is that! And we are here in prison, I, for self-defense, is this justice? Obviously not. That's why I have little regard to the laws as they are now. I go by what is moral and not by what is "lawful", and so should everyone do that wishes to be just and moral."

"Like the ancient Greeks said: abide by the laws only when you must, and if the laws are corrupt, and you want to change the laws, then go and take power."

"That sums things nicely, the people, the hard working and decent people, need to have real power in their OWN state."

"Yes."

And so we ended out discourse with that very important conclusion.

PART X

Some days passed, there wasn't much action here, where only sick and wounded people dwelt.

The building we were in was near the building where those who were mentally challenged were kept – we used to hear their screams at night. It wasn't very scary, just yells, I guess, for no reason – but maybe there was some dark reason behind these mad screams.

Also, someone, not very old, died in our wing. In his last days he used to complain a lot for pains and for not being able to breath. The doctors and paramedics didn't take him seriously for several days but then his condition got rapidly worse. He was taken to the hospital, brought back, and something like a day later he died. What a horrible death to die like that in prison.

While being there and spending my days I found a little

conversational book in Spanish, so I started to learn Spanish, I didn't have anything better to do after all. And by some strange luck some 10 days after I picked up this book a new guy came, 23 years old, from Argentina. He was not in the same room as me at first, but with the former hitman, but they didn't get along, so when the old man in my room got released the argentine boy came to our room, and we became good friends, actually he was the best company I had there. And a day later another man from the hitman's room came; he also didn't get along with him (most people didn't). He was 65 years old, but looked 20 years younger, and he liked to workout. He was at the end of his 20 years long sentence and unfortunately got ill at the very last months. He was a good man (albeit also a murderer) and he knew a lot of things, cooking, handiness, and the like. A very useful roommate and a great company.

With these 2 and with the other friends I made from the other cells I was really happy there.

The old man who got released left me a radio, I got books, there was a television, a comfortable bed, and a relatively decent food and in plenty, and some board games. With all this and good fun friends, life in prison weren't so bad. Actually it was quite nice: having all your day free, watching movies, reading, listening to music, talking and laughing.

Of course, this wasn't proper jail; it was meant for the sick and injured. There wasn't even a dungeon (I will get to know the dungeon very well some while later, when I'll be moved to other prisons).

The argentine boy told me about his country and his house, how living costs were very high there compared to the average salary, and how he had to steal just to survive.

He came to Israel together with his girlfriend and she also was in prison – same prison compound but a different prison, for women. He told me about her and about his family, how he rented a house, a big one with a private pool, and had 4 cats and 3 dogs waiting for him at home.

His life in argentine sounded quite nice. Perhaps in some countries and in some situations it pays to steal?

He didn't know Hebrew, except for a very few words, so we communicated mostly in English, with some Spanish, as far as I could. Though I learned fast, Spanish isn't a hard language to learn.

But did you ever noticed how, in every language, there are times that you want to say something, express a thought, share ideas that you want to express, and you can't find the right words ?

That in our languages there are not enough words to express certain ideas, usually more deep and sublime ideas, but not necessarily. And so we are forced to express ourselves in the same old pattern of speech, and in this pattern we also think our conscious thoughts, and so we lose many higher thoughts, thoughts we were unable to process just because we didn't have the right words to express them to ourselves and to others. I wonder how much knowledge has passed away just because of this shortcoming in our languages.

We might have had a better understanding of ourselves, the world and others if we didn't have to give up certain lines of thought, just because we don't know, and don't have, the right words to express them.

Take for example the word good, it has many meanings, some are deep, but we are forced to always use the same word for different ideas. That confuses us and our hearers and limits us if we want to express something different, unusual.

Good, may be referring to something that is good – good for something. Good as in the opposite of bad. Good, as an approval, good as best, good as the opposite of evil (bad and evil are not the same), good to express comfort, satisfaction, even cynicism – you use the same word for different ideas and so you are limited to this word and to its general and most common meaning.

That's how many misunderstandings of our ideas may occur, and you can notice this especially when you try to communicate with someone in a foreign language, and especially when both of you talk in a language that is foreign to you, like when I was talking with my argentine friend.

My friend was young but quite intelligent. Perhaps he used to read some books before he landed in prison. Though, you can get more intelligent by reading books IN prison.

My friend was also a catholic Christian, though not a very believing man. And my other roommate was a believing Jew.

Oh, and by the way, the first roommate I had, that came with me from the other room (I'm sure you remember), the former firefighter, he was released to a house arrest. We had also another roommate, a half burned man (seriously!), he was kind of quiet and didn't talk much about himself, I only knew that he was there for murder because during a fight with the firefighter he tried to scare him with him being a murderer (he succeeded), but still he was a very skinny half-burned man, one little push and he was down – the firefighter was a bulky man.

So basically we were me, the old man that looked and

behaved younger (it's even weird to call him an old man), the argentine boy and the half burned man, that kept for himself. He was not a very good company and used to ask us to be more quiet when we were telling stories and laughing- so from now on I'll keep quiet about him – as a sort of quiet revenge.

So, the three of us were chatting as usual, the argentine boy just came from a meeting with a catholic nun, she checked on him and asked how he was doing. Also, she gave him a call card (300 minutes in Israel but only 60 minutes if you called abroad), and helped connect and pass messages between him and his girlfriend, and between them and their embassy. The only thing she asked was for him and his girlfriend to remain chaste till they got married – that made him laugh, he was not very chaste, not even with regard to his girlfriend. Still, he said that as the nun was very nice and helping he will do his best.

All this nun business made us think of religion, more aware that we had grown up under different religious influences.

"So, are you going to be more religious now?" I asked.

"Maybe, it's important to follow the rules of religion."

"Do you think? What is so good about it?"

"I don't know, it's important, that's the basic thing of moralily, if people won't follow the rules of religion everyone will do what they want without any regard to laws and morals."

"there are so many people, even here, and those you read about in the news, in history books, and the people you meet in your everyday-life, people that follow their religious creed and yet they are far from moral in their private life, they steal, cheat, kill, betray and so on…"

Here my other roommate had to say a word, being somewhat religious himself: "then these people arc not really religious people. They just pretend to be so to reach their own private ends. Real religious people are just and moral men, and that's right for all religions, even for Islam."

"You touched a spot here, in Islam indeed there are many deeds of terror and violence, claimed to be done for god and religion. So can you kill children and innocent citizens in the name of religion?"

"No, of course not, those that do it (or preach it) are just hypocrites, they either don't understand religion altogether or they use it to achieve their own ends.

God doesn't want us to kill each other, but rather to live in harmony, follow his rules, and be good to ourselves and to others."

"Yes, that's what many Islamists say, those that are more quiet, more in the background. They might be the majority of Islamists, but like in many other instances, it's the more violent, noisy and aggressive minority that is on the forefront, and people might mistake them for the majority- while they are only a radical minority."

"I have known many islamists here in prison. They don't smoke, don't drink, they quietly pray 5 times a day, and are generally good people."

"So if people that follow true religion are usually

peaceful and moral, how did all the wars and massacres caused by religion came about?"

"You both said it", said the argentine "violent people, a violent minority, used religion to achieve their own ends. If you read about the introduction of Christianity to the roman world you see just that: the first Christians were peaceful, and practiced their religion humbly and in peace. They obeyed the state laws, and when the laws forbade them to practice their religion they quietly accepted tortures and death, they never revolted, and they believed that all their sufferings here are for god and that they will be rewarded for their piety and honest religious spirit in an afterlife to come.

But when Christianity became the ruling religion, then they used religion to destroy their enemies, in the most brutal ways possible. Every province had their own sect of Christianity and they slaughtered each other, in the name, or at least by the excuse, of destroying the enemies of god.

Sometimes they barely even used an excuse, like in the story of the Borgias- using religion in a cynical way to get power and wealth."

"True. Religion is still being used that way, and apparently will be used like this for many years more. But the role of religion is slowly weakening; some say that the new religion is science, since people must have some religion in their life. In a way, that might be true.

Some say that people don't follow the rules of religion and that's why we see people becoming less and less moral. That might be also true – actually it is true in many respects.

But as far as I can see the real god of our time is money. People shamelessly follow and admire money now, and those that have plenty of it.

Of course that always was like this, but in our days it's much more pronounced. Money has taken the place of god, even for those that say they worship god, and you can see the influence of this old-new god everywhere in our society."

"Real religion still exist", said my roommate, "but as you both said those that follow it falsely are in the forefront, but there is still a pious majority that believes and follow god."

"And do you truly believe in god?"

"Yes I do. God has created man and all other things. Everything was made for a purpose by god, though we often can't see the true purpose of things. But god guides us, everyone of us, to our true path in life."

"Do you think that it's really god's business to watch and guide you, and also other people?"

"Yes I do. The world was created for us, and when we leave this world our souls, which are divine, will return to god."

Here the argentine boy had to say something: "but don't you think that god has anything better to do?"

"Indeed", I said "it's quite absurd to think that your little daily life is the primary concern of god. If god is divine this things should not be so all-important to him. It's absurd to think of god as a petty old man that watches every deed or thought that you might have, and then dispense either punishment or reward as he sees fit.

It's a sort of blasphemy to think of god as a being whose total thought is concerned with your little prayers and your daily life."

"Not at all", said the religious man, "god wants us to pray and follow his laws. We don't pray for god but for ourselves. And yes, god watches us as his children."

"I still think it's absurd to imagine god having nothing to do but to watch out petty deeds.

And anyway I don't agree with how religion sees god.

God is angry, punishing, rewarding, happy, sad: really like a human, but god is not a human, he should be a higher being beyond our comprehension. All human feelings like love, hate, envy, anger are being given to god as if he is a mere human, only with absolute power.

It shows you how primitive the belief in god is.

I think that in the beginning people could not explain many things that happened to them like death, drought, floods, fires and the like. So they imagined that there were in nature some invisible powerful beings, like themselves in nature, which were angry at them.

This helped them to explain the world around them and also to get rid of the dreaded randomness of life: by praying, ceremonies and sacrifices they could appease these beings and so avert these random disasters.

That's really how religions were created, by the need of humans to have a cause for what they can't otherwise explain, to get rid of the dreaded and unexplained randomness, and to have power and control over things, by having a god to appease, to ask, and to pray to, so that god (nature) will do as people ask of him.

So in reality gods were made as a way for humans to feel they have control over their environment, to get rid of this horrible notion that things were random and you may live happily one day and be wiped out the next day, like an ant or any other animal. But that's reality, people just don't want to accept it, they can't accept it.

One more thing humans won't accept is death, so they created an afterlife and a soul – again just to feel they have power over life, that they don't just randomly die and disappear like the rest of the animals, but that they have a special destiny to live on, to have a purpose.

So that's why god was created: so that people will feel as if they have control over their environment and over randomness, and to relieve their fear of death and ending. And also to flatter themselves as special beings: god thinks of them day and night, the world and the other animals were created for them. Nonsense! People just won't accept that they are not so special, that they are just like any other animal, that life can be random, and that there are many things in the universe that they don't understand.

Even non-religious people still have to believe that they are special, that science gives them total control over their lives. Both these assumptions are not true: 1. Science is still very limited and can't control our environment and nature to a large degree.

2. We are completely like any other animal, just that after long years of evolution we have reached the stage where we can pass our knowledge to the next generations with ease through language. That's the secret of our advancement over other animals, that we can build on the knowledge and experience of all the other generations

before us instead of having to discover the same things again and again every generation – that's how we have advanced faster in the last few thousand years, after some 1.5 millions of years since the human race has come into being. Without reaching the stage where we can pass our knowledge and experience with ease through language we would not have changed much beyond primitive man- still using sticks and stones, and having our discoveries remain limited to the use of these tools over and over again, every new generation, like a bird that builds a nest and a monkey that uses a stick to fish ants from their nests."

"So do you prefer to believe that god doesn't care about us, and that we are not different than monkeys and ants, that we have no souls and that we just die and disappear?"

"Yes, I do prefer to see the world like this. But it's not a matter of preference, that's reality, and we must boldly face the truth instead of having fantasies about life.

But anyway I think it's a good thing we are not so special, having no souls, no after life, and no special purpose.

This gives us a huge freedom, the freedom to find the meaning to our lives, without constrains and without imaginary rules. We can make our own purpose in life and see life as a game.

I do see life as a game and I know that whether I win or lose it will end the same for all of us. And its I who choose what is my goal and what it means to win. Is it not a huge freedom? To make your own destiny, and not to be afraid of imaginary influences?"

"I'm not sure, if what you say is true then there is no purpose to life, so what's the point in living then?

If we are like ants and nothing is important in us we can live or die and it won't matter much- so what's the purpose?"

"You have to choose your purpose in life. Do you need to be the center of the universe to have a purpose in your life?

Just be sure in one thing: if god exists he is a God not an all-powerful man, so don't fix on him any notions of anger or care for your own little private life.

I know that some religious people say that god is all and is also nothing. I see it as : god is everything that exists but he is nothing with a purpose, no anger, no love, no envy, no care- these are human, not divine feelings.

So whether there is or there isn't a god is irrelevant to us, we live our own lives, our own random and unimportant lives, yea, like ants, and we choose, or ought to choose, what is the purpose and goal of our individual lives."

So we ended our discourse.

PART XI

We had a few more days together till the argentine boy had to leave, and was transferred to a regular jail, as he was already healed from his operation.

It was sad to see him leave but he was soon to end his sentence, which was quite short, and then he would be expelled back to Argentina together with his girlfriend.

As a foreign subject his sentence was quite short and on top of that he got a third off automatically. That's makes sense - the state of Israel had no interest to keep him captive, they preffered to send him back to his country instead of letting him stay here as a liability – maintaining a captive in prison require resources after all.

Just when he left another guy came to replace him (that's how it was in prison- very crowded, so every bed was occupied).

This new guy was a 7 times Israeli wrestling champion, though his career ended some while ago because of a motorcycle accident.

As you might guess he was in prison for hitting someone till he was unconscious. And the reason why he was in the prison's infirmary was because he had a fight with someone in prison, and this brave someone splashed him with boiling water (a known practice in prison).

The new guy was actually quite nice and not as bellicose as you might expect. He quickly became fond of the former hitman and liked to spend his time with him. He actually was a nice guy and he smiled a lot.

After only a few days he left, together with his beloved hitman, which also had to go to a regular prison, a thing he wanted to be able to do long before- he was used to prison.

I had (I actually hadn't – but they told me I had so I had to go half way and then come back) a court meeting the same day so I was leaving with them.

We finally parted, somewhat sadly, when it was time for us to take a separate jail-transport bus (known locally as "Posta").

When I came back after a vain trip to nowhere another guy came to our room. He was in the hitman's room before that.

This guy was quite nice and quiet. When I asked him what brought him to prison he said that he stabbed his neighbor and a cop and asked me whether I didn't see it on the news. I said I didn't but later on I remembered I actually did, just that it was a month ago so I didn't really remembered it on the spot. But even now I can remember how they showed the trail of blood- lots of blood- that his neighbor left behind as he escaped for his life down the stairs. I wondered how he could have escaped alive after losing so much blood.

The new guy said his neighbor was so scared and shocked that he escaped, leaving his girlfriend behind. But it's hard to judge him as long as we weren't in the same situation.

Sounds kind of scary isn't it? But as I told you the guy was quite nice and quiet. I know that I heard many times that those that are the most quiet are also capable to be the most dangerous. But anyway, from my experience he was a nice guy with a nice talent for drawing.

So a few more days passed, the new guy was a bit depressed and lied in bed most of the time and didn't talk much- you could understand him, he was in prison and was also shot 3 times. So I could mostly talk only with my other roommate. We had some interesting chats and I still enjoyed my time, though we had less laughter since the argentine boy left.

One day I was told by the prison's doctor that as my condition improved I too will be soon moved to a regular prison.

I was sad at the news and a bit anxious too, since a regular prison should be tougher. But I was also somewhat curious, and to tell the truth, as much as I had a nice time in the jail infirmary and was as relaxed as I could be there, it was after all a very small place, and very quiet, and yea, I kind of started to get bored there. So I received the doctor's news with mixed feelings.

But the thing is I didn't really recover and I shouldn't have been released from the infirmary, as the operation I have been through was apparently not so well done, the area that was stitched started to open up from the inside.

After I left the infirmary and was in a regular prison I had a hell of troubles to get the prison's authorities to treat this problem, and it took more than 6 months (!) till I had my second operation, that should have been done immediately. And in this time it got worse and worse. But on these troubles later. Though as you might know, prison isn't a good place to be physically weak.

For now I only felt a bit of sad to leave behind the friends that I made here, knowing I won't see them again.

Just a bit before I left I saw my friend (the one with the long sentence that had a room by himself in the secluded section) with a bandage around his left foot.

Asking him what happened he told me he had a gangrene. Asking him why it happened he said that he stopped to take all of his 31-32 pills, and that now he could die anytime from a stroke or a heart attack. I immediately saw what he was planning – a suicide of sorts. He was tired of prison and had no hope of building a new life 9 years later when he got released – it's hard, getting into prison in his 20's and leaving an old man 60 years old in a sick body. I saw his point but still tried to dissuade him, I was sad on his account.

But being in his place, I don't know whether I would have had any hope. After all he missed all his life in prison, and his health too.

He was put in a secluded prison some time ago, for 4 years – as a sort of punishment. 4 years only by himself in his cell. That partly broke him.

So was he right in his choice?

It's hard to answer it. He has lost all hope of achieving anything in his life, or to build any life that is worth living.

But does it matter if he lives or dies? Does he lose anything if he sees no hope and choose to end his life?

What will he gain by the continuation of his life? Or what will he lose by ending them earlier that they would have ended?

Actually he would have gained nothing if he continued to live, only misery, and he lost nothing in ending his life sooner, except the pain of dying, which any of us will experience sooner or later (I have already experienced it twice, having the luck of being close to death twice in my life).

So what can you gain from life? Nothing of real absolute importance, since in the end you and all those around you will die. All that you have done will disappear and become irrelevant. And if you die early? You just end the game earlier, the result doesn't matter.

Or does it?

If we look at our lives from a very high perspective then life is worthless, we lumber in vain and our lives are exactly the same- has the same meaning as we give to the life, and unceasing labor, of an ant.

But why do we need to look at our lives from the perspective of the boundless cosmos. Of course that in the end humanity is no more than an ant colony, but we need to look at our lives from OUR OWN perspective.

And from our perspective our lives does matter and our goals in life are important (so are also the goals of the ant).

But if we don't achieve them? Then life is a game, we lost, and the game is over. And if we do achieve our goals? Then we win and the game is over.

As you see, it's over this way or that, so the end comes either way.

That makes life a game and our goals the objective. If we don't like the game that's ok, you can retire and quit the game. Or you can play and try to reach your goal. Just don't take this game too seriously because whether you win or lose the game is over and the result is forgotten.

Maybe we will return and play the same game over and

over again and maybe not. But I can offer you one good advice and it is this: it's just a game!

Epilogue

So the day came when I was to leave the prison's infirmary.

I was told about the day only the night before (they always did it), so I had no time to say goodbye to everyone since the cells were already closed for the night.

I packed most of my things and went to sleep with mixed feelings, somewhat sad to leave this comfortable place and the friends I made here. And somewhat excited so see how real prison would be like.

In the early morning, 5 AM, I was waken up and told to be ready. I said goodbye to my roommates, we parted, even hugged. It was a bit sad.

I got outside of our wing's building to the next building, where my stuff was checked. Then I had to board an armored jail bus, with other people that were also to be transported somewhere (to another prison like me, or to court).

The road was dreary and grey and cold (it was early morning in April). It took an hour long.

We got to our station and slowly went inside (there were many security checks at the entrance to each prison, even when it was in the same prison compound).

Those of us that were to move to this prison climbed down the armored jail bus.

The place was grey, dark and unclean. Very different from the place I came from, which had to be hygienic because of the sick and wounded that lived there.

Now I have come to a real prison and new, tougher, adventures were about to begin.

Thank you for purchasing this book and reading it to the very end. The story is not finished though...

If you liked this book then please take a few minutes to write a review in amazon. It would help me a lot and motivate me towards writing the sequel.

If you have any questions, or have any ideas you would like to share, you can write to me at:

Dabaryela1@gmail.com

I would like to hear from you, and I'll do my best to answer each and every one of your questions or comments.

Made in the USA
Coppell, TX
01 November 2020

40556625R00069